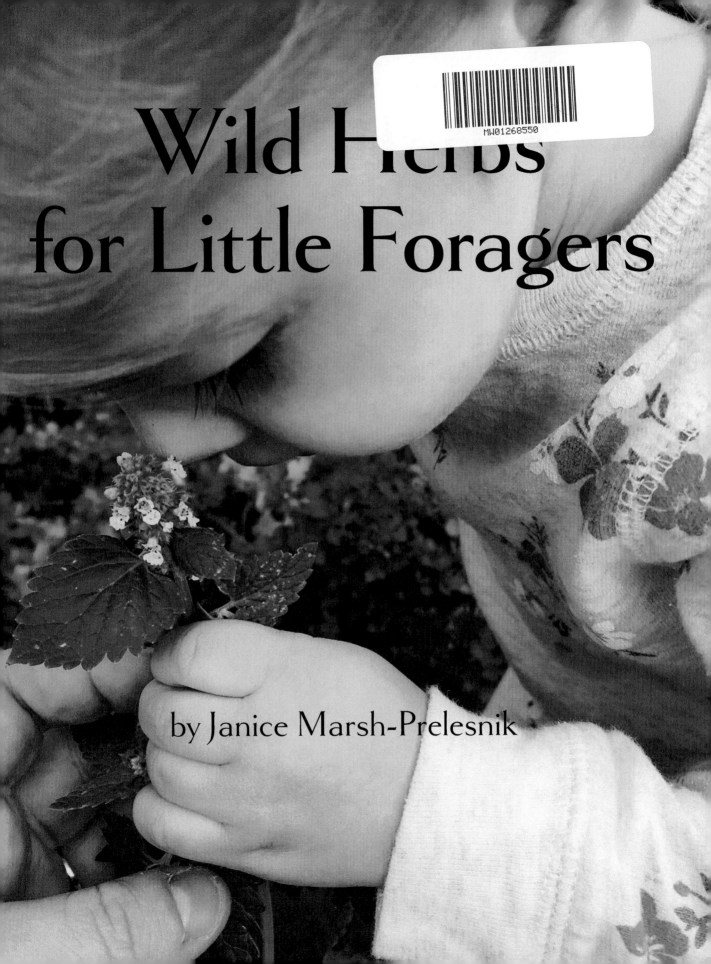

Wild Herbs
for Little Foragers

by Janice Marsh-Prelesnik

ISBN-13:
978-1717220301

ISBN-10:
1717220304

Disclaimer: The information in this book is traditional knowledge passed down from generation to generation and is in no way medical advice.

Author: Janice Marsh-Prelesnik © 2018
Book layout: Allison McKenna

Wild Herbs
for Little Foragers

This book belongs to:

_____

A Song for the Earth
(sung to the ABC tune)

Oh the earth is good to me
And so I thank the earth kindly
For giving me the things I need
The ground for me to plant some seeds
The earth is good, so good to me
She will take good care of me!

Wild Herbs
for Little Foragers

This book is for my adored frolicking foragers, Adela, Davick, Emilia, and Cadence. May you always cherish and defend Grandmother Earth and the plants she provides. You are Grandma GJ's legacy.

Legacy - something that happens or exists as a result of things that happened at an earlier time.

Safety Checklist

I, _____ promise to:

- Never put any plant in my mouth unless I have been taught that it is a safe plant for me to eat.

- When using hot water I will have a big person help me.

- Pay close attention to the plants around me and make sure that I am not touching any plant that can hurt me.

- Be sure that the plants are not contaminated.

Being a Friend of the Earth and the Plants Checklist

I, _____ promise to:

- Use the plants that I harvest.

- I will not harvest all of the plants in one area.

- Be thankful for the gifts of plants.

- Have permission before I collect plants.

Trickster Plants to Avoid

Poison Ivy

My name is poison ivy. Most people dislike me very, very much! My leaves have oil on the surface that can make you have a blistery rash that itches a few hours after you touch it. If you happen to touch me you can wash your skin for several minutes with soap and warm water. This will wash the oil off your skin which can help to prevent the itchy rash.

People say that I don't have any purpose growing on the earth. I disagree! My purpose is to teach you how to pay attention and look closely at the plant world. If you learn to pay close attention to your surroundings you will know not to touch me.

Here is how you can identify me—My leaves are in groups of three and are pointy and smooth on the edges with a notch on the side leaves. I can grow on the ground or I can be a vine and climb up a tree. When I grow up a tree my stem has fuzzy rootlets; these help me attach strongly to the tree. I have clusters of white berries in the fall. My leaves are reddish in the spring, and then turn green, and then turn red again in the fall.

Here is a poem to help you remember what I look like:

No matter what time of year,
Be sure that you stay clear,
If you see leaves in groups of three,
One, two, three, let them be!
Hairy vine, no friend of mine.
Berries white, danger in sight.

Stilfehler (https://commons.wikimedia.org/wiki/File:Poison_Ivy_Leaves.jpg),
"Poison Ivy Leaves", https://creativecommons.org/licenses/by-sa/3.0/legalcode

⚠ REMEMBER: If you touch poison ivy or poison oak go and wash the area with soap and warm water for several minutes. Also, change your clothes and make sure an adult washes them as soon as possible. The oil from Poison Ivy and Poison Oak can stick to clothes as well as your body!

Poison Oak

Hello there! I am poison oak. My friend, poison ivy
and I both like to play tricks on you! I also can make
you very itchy if you rub up against my leaves. Like
poison ivy I have groups of three leaves which are
either green or reddish colored and white berries. You
can tell us apart because my leaves are wavy instead
of pointy like poison ivy. You can find me growing as a
shrub, or climbing vine.

Eeekster (https://commons.wikimedia.org/wiki/File:Poison-oak-flowering.jpg),
"Poison-oak-flowering", https://creativecommons.org/licenses/by-sa/3.0/legalcode

Rose

Please be gentle and go slow when smelling my beautiful
flower and be careful to not grab my stem! I have sharp thorns
on my stems that feel like a bee sting when you touch them.
When I grow in the wild I look like a bush. My rose petals
taste good as a tea or fresh in a salad. The fruit, called a rose
hip, is also tasty in tea.

Black Raspberry

I am black raspberry. Like my cousin, rose, I also have thorns on my stems. My berries are good to eat, but be careful when you pick them. Watch out for the thorns! You can also make a tea with my leaves. I like to grow at the edge of woods.

Stinging Nettle

Last but not least, be on the lookout for me, stinging nettle. People like to eat my leaves and make tea from my leaves as they are very healthy for you. How am I a trickster? I have little hairs on my stems that sting you when you touch them. Ouch!

I grow in big patches and can grow up to six feet tall. That's as tall, or taller, as your adults! I like sun or part shade.

Violet photos by Krystal Gast.

Violet

Hello friends. Happy spring to all of you! My name is Violet. I am one of the first plants that you will find in the springtime. I'm not really fussy about where I live. You might find me along the edge of woods or in the corner of your back yard. Full sun or part shade; I don't really care. I am just so happy to have emerged from my winter underground home. Sometimes I have purple flowers and sometimes my flowers are white or yellow. My flowers smell and taste sweet.

Look at my photo carefully. Did you notice that I have five flower petals? Two are on top and three are on the bottom. The white dot in the center helps bees know where to go to find my sweet nectar. My leaves are heart shaped and toothed, which means they are jagged along the edges.

When you have a sore throat and/or cough, my flowers and leaves can help you feel better. For an infusion pick a handful of leaves and flowers and put them in a cup. Have an adult pour hot water in the teacup. Simmer for 10-15 minutes or longer for stronger medicine. Strain out the leaves and flowers and sip away.

Violet Infused Honey

1. Fill a glass jar with my leaves and flowers.
2. Then fill the jar with honey.
3. Let the leaves and flowers infuse, or sit in the honey, for three to four weeks.
4. When the infusion is done strain the flowers and leaves out of the honey.
5. Yum, violet honey is so good with hot tea!

Violet (Viola sp.)

You can tape a plant pressing on this page, draw your own plant, or make a rubbing of the plant.

Where did you find Violet?

Found in meadows and edges of woods. Flowers can be violet, white or yellow. 6" tall when fully grown.

Dandelion

Greetings, my friends! I am Dandelion. My name means lion's tooth because my leaves are pointy and jagged like the teeth of a lion. I like to pretend that my flowers are the sun, my seed puff is the moon, and my seeds flying in the wind are shooting stars. So many people misunderstand me. They try to chase me away out of their lawns. I won't give up though! I hope that once I tell my story people will once again see how kind and helpful I can be. In the early springtime you can pick my leaves and eat them in your salad. Or you can be like the rabbits and just nibble on a leaf when you are outside playing.

You can also eat my flower petals. Take them off one by one and put them in your salad.

Mini Dandelion Pancakes

Ingredients:
- 2 cups dandelion flowers, rinsed
- 1 1/4 cups flour
- 1 egg
- 1 cup milk of any kind
- Olive oil, or butter

Combine flour, egg and milk and mix well. You can add a little more flour if you want your batter to be thicker. Heat oil in skillet. Dip dandelion flower heads into batter until completely covered and lay into skillet. Cook just like pancakes! Serve warm with syrup, honey or applesauce.

Dandelion (Taraxacum officinale)

You can tape a plant pressing on this page, draw your own plant, or make a rubbing of the plant.

Where did you find Dandelion?

Found in lawns, gardens, meadows, roadsides. Flower head grows 1-2", flowering stalk is 12" up to 18", leaves grow close to ground.

Chickweed

Well hello there! I am chickweed. You are welcome to pick some of my leaves and eat them. Put me in a salad along with my friend Violet flower. Lots of animals like to eat me too! You can pretend that you are a mouse eating me for dinner.

I like to spread out on the ground. With my little oval shaped leaves and tiny star flowers I can be easy to miss. You will find me spread low to the ground and I often plant myself in the vegetable garden or flower beds. I like cool weather, so better eat me now before it gets too hot. I can even grow under the snow. Every night my leaves fold over tender buds and shoots like a blanket to keep the flower buds warm.

```
            Chickweed Smoothie


Ingredients


1 1/2 cups plain yogurt
1 cup chopped fresh young chickweed
2  cups chopped fresh or frozen fruit
1 avocado, chunked


Blend until smooth.
```

Chickweed (Stellaria media)

You can tape a plant pressing on this page, draw your own plant, or make a rubbing of the plant.

Where did you find Chickweed?

Found in gardens and open ground. Stems are ½ to-1' long and sprawls across the ground. Leaves are opposite on green or burgundy stems.

Broadleaf Plantain

Broadleaf Plantain is my name, helping is my game! It's true, I can be helpful to you if you ever get stung by a bee, or mosquito, or have a sliver. If these things happen to you, you can make a poultice from my leaf. All you do is pick one of my leaves, rub it between your hands, and then place it on the sting, bite or the sliver. Hold it there and soon you will feel better.

Remember the trickster plants? If you ever are bothered by a poison ivy rash, nettle sting or burn I can help these problems feel better too! Just rub my leaf and then hold it on your skin. You can also make a compress with me. Here is how: make a strong infusion with my leaf, strain the leaf out of the water, get a cloth wet with the tea and then hold the cloth on your skin. Make sure the water is cooled before you put it on your skin!

```
        Plantain Poultice and Compress

Poultice--place a fresh plantain leaf  right
on the skin.

Compress--make a strong infusion by pouring
boiled water over a handful of plantain
leaves.  After infusion has cooled, dip the
cloth in the infusion, wring out  and place on
skin.
```

Broadleaf Plantain (Plantago major)

You can tape a plant pressing on this page, draw your own plant, or make a rubbing of the plant.

Where did you find Broadleaf Plantain?

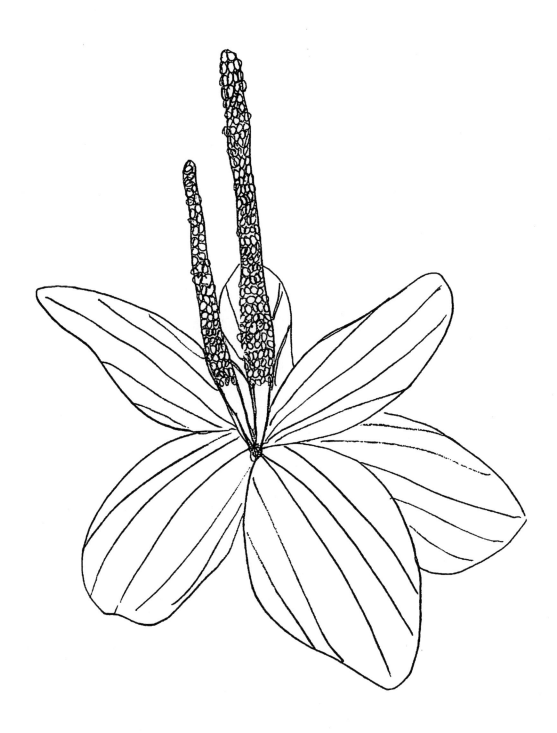

Found in lawns and gardens, sun or part shade. Unbranched flower stalks are 4"-20" tall and grow from the center of the leaves which are 2-5" long and 1½–3" across. Leaves are oval in shape with about 5 parallel veins.

Wood Sorrel

Wood Sorrel is my name, but sometimes people call me Sourgrass. They call me this because my leaves, flowers and stems taste sour, like a lemon. My heart shaped leaves grow in groups of three. My tiny flowers are usually yellow but can be white as well. You can nibble on me raw or drink me in a tea. It makes me happy to grow in people's gardens.

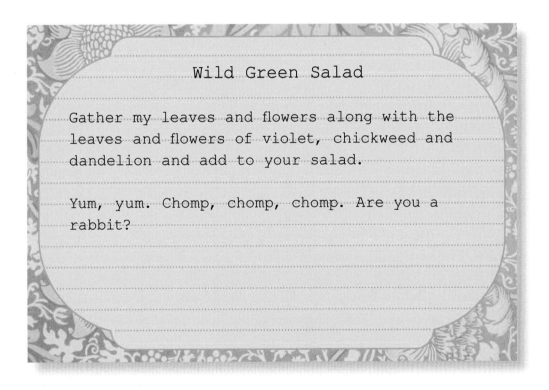

```
          Wild Green Salad


Gather my leaves and flowers along with the
leaves and flowers of violet, chickweed and
dandelion and add to your salad.

Yum, yum. Chomp, chomp, chomp. Are you a
rabbit?
```

Wood Sorrel (Oxalis stricta)

You can tape a plant pressing on this page, draw your own plant, or make a rubbing of the plant.

Where did you find Wood Sorrel?

This edible plant usually grows to between 3-8 inches high.
Wood sorrel prefers moist soil, and partial shade and can be found in the woods or shady areas near the garden and homes.

Red Clover

I am Red Clover. Come on over and nibble on my tasty little flowers. Be careful, though! The honey bees love me too. In fact, I am proud to say that some of the best honey is made from my flowers. Like bees, butterflies also love to sip my nectar. Cows, horses and deer love to eat me as well.

You can find me along the highways, but please remember not to eat my flowers if they are near roads as they are not very clean. Instead look for me in gardens or in meadows. If you have a bad cough red clover tea can help you feel better. People say my friend peppermint and my flowers go well together in a cough tea.

My leaves are pointed and have white marks in the middle that help bees find their way to the flowers. If you look very carefully you may find a group of four leaves. Some people believe a four leaf clover brings you good luck!

My flower head has a lot of flowers on it. You can pick off each one to nibble on.

Red Clover Blossom Sun Tea

Ingredients:
1-2 cups of fresh red clover blossoms
1 quart of water

Directions:
Add flowers to a 1-quart mason jar. Pour the water over the herbs & let sit in the sun all day. Strain & enjoy.
If you don't drink all the tea at once you can keep this tea in the refrigerator for 2-3 days.

Red Clover (Trifolium pratense)

You can tape a plant pressing on this page, draw your own plant, or make a rubbing of the plant.

Where did you find Red Clover?

Grows ½'-2' tall in full sun. Found in fields, meadows, grassy areas

Catnip

I'm crazy Catnip. Do you have a cat? Give your cat some of my leaves and watch him/her start acting crazy! Most cats love to munch on my leaves, as it makes them act silly and playful. I don't have this effect on people but if made into a tea, I can help you if your stomach hurts.

If you rub my leaves on your skin it may keep some mosquitoes and bugs away.
My jagged leaves grow opposite of one another and are soft and fuzzy. I have a group of small white flowers that grow at the top of me. My stems are square because I am from the mint family. Do you know a cat that loves catnip? You can dry some catnip so it can be enjoyed all winter long! Here is how:

Dry Catnip

Directions:
1. Cut off two or three stems near the bottom of the plant.
2. Gently shake the plant so that any insects that may be on the leaves fall off.
3. Wrap a rubber band around the stems near the bottom where the cut is.
4. Hang this upside down in a warm, dark place. A closet or cupboard works well.
5. When the leaves are dry and crispy take them off the stems and store them in a container.   MEOW!!!

Catnip (Nepata cataria)

You can tape a plant pressing on this page, draw your own plant, or make a rubbing of the plant.

Where did you find Catnip?

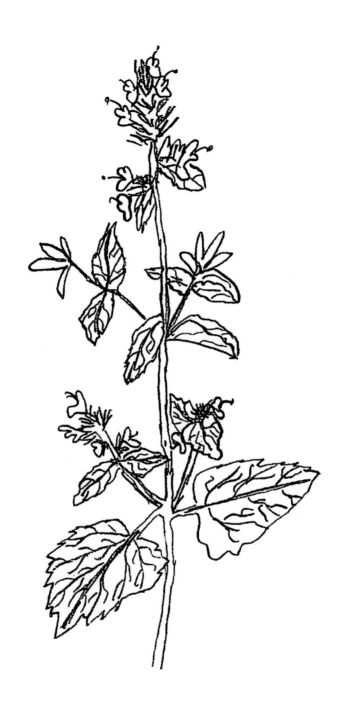

Grows 1-4' tall, full sun or partial shade. Found in open ground, meadows, fields, gardens.

Lemon Balm

Hello there. My name is Lemon Balm. Did you notice how much I look like my cousin, Catnip? Our flowers are very similar and so are the shapes of our leaves. My stems are also square shaped because, like catnip, I am from the mint family.

If you look closely you can see our differences—My leaves are a lighter shade of green and they are not fuzzy like Catnip's leaves. What do you smell when you rub my leaves together? Do you smell lemon? Of course, this is why I am named Lemon Balm. The word balm means soothing. That is my claim to fame. If you are feeling grouchy or scared you can drink tea made from my leaves. I can help you feel more relaxed.

Lemon Balm Fruit Salad

Chop up a few lemon balm leaves
and sprinkle on a fruit salad.
Lemon balm tastes especially good
on watermelon!

Lemon Balm (Melissa officinalis)

You can tape a plant pressing on this page, draw your own plant, or make a rubbing of the plant.

Where did you find Lemon Balm?

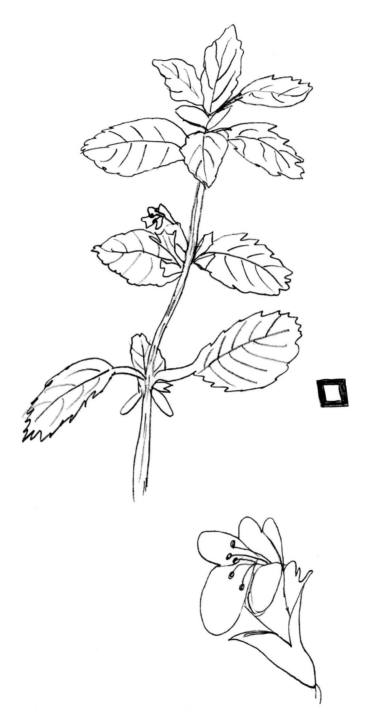

Grows up to 1' tall. Escaped from gardens. Loves to grow next to homes and in gardens.

Yarrow photos by Krystal Gast

46

Yarrow

Hi friends—My name is Yarrow and I have super powers! If you happen to get a small cut you can put some of my leaves and flowers on the cut which will help to stop bleeding. Like my friend plantain, I can also help stings and burns feel better as well.

My flowers bloom in the summertime. I have clusters of 15 to 40 tiny disk flowers on each stem. My lacey leaves spiral around my stem. People often infuse my leaves and flowers in oil and then make a salve from the yarrow oil. You can also combine me with plantain for a super power salve!

```
                    Yarrow Salve

    1.   Fill a jar with yarrow leaves and flowers
    2.   Add olive oil, fill to the top
    3.   Let sit for 3-5 weeks (Make sure that all
         of the plant is covered with oil. Check
         daily and add more oil if needed.)
    4.   Strain the plant from the oil.
    5.   Melt ¼ cup beeswax to 1 cup of yarrow oil.
         Make sure an adult helps with this.)
    6.   Place in jar and let harden at room
         temperature.
```

Yarrow (Achillia millefolium)

You can tape a plant pressing on this page, draw your own plant, or make a rubbing of the plant.

Where did you find Yarrow?

Grows 1'-3' tall, usually in dry ground. Blooms late spring through fall. Likes full sun.

Echinacea photo by Janice Marsh-Prelesnik.

Echinacea photo by Janice Marsh-Prelesnik.

Purple Coneflower

A-choo! Feel like you may be coming down with a cold? I can help that sickness go away! I am Echinacea and I have special powers that can wake up white blood cells that help get rid of the pesky bacteria that are trying to make you sick. I can help prevent an illness the most at the beginning, so please listen to what your body tells you!

My name means hedgehog, because my seed cones are bristly and pokey. My flowers range from light to dark pink and my alternate leaves are pointed. I love the hot summer days! Do you?

You can drink my flowers, leaves and roots in an infusion or as a tincture. When you drink me you will feel a tingly feeling on your tongue. That tingle tells you that my medicine is on its way to waking up your white blood cells! You can make a glycerin tincture yourself! Here is how:

Echinacea Glycerin Tincture

1. Chop flowers and leaves and place in a small jar.
2. Cover with a mixture of one part vegetable glycerin to one part water.
3. Infuse flowers and leaves until it gets cold in the fall.
4. When it is cold, dig up roots and wash and dry them.
5. Separate the flowers and leaves from glycerin.
6. Chop up roots and add to glycerin.
7. Let set for 4 weeks.

Separate roots from glycerin.
Take 10-15 drops hourly when you feel a sickness is coming on.

Purple Coneflower (Echinacea purpurea)

You can tape a plant pressing on this page, draw your own plant, or make a rubbing of the plant.

Where did you find Purple Coneflower?

Grows up to 3' in sunny open meadows and gardens. Flowers in midsummer through fall.

Mullein photos by Krystal Gast.

54

Mullein

I am Mullein and I stand for courage and strength! Stand tall and strong with me, my friend! My silvery green leaves are very fuzzy and grow around one another in a circle. When I am two years old I send up a huge flower stalk with bright yellow flowers. I can help you in many ways--you can drink a tea of my leaves to help keep your lungs strong. Make sure you strain the tea very well so the fuzzy parts of my leaves are strained away, otherwise the fuzzy parts can make your throat scratchy.

My flowers can help you if you have an earache. To make an earache remedy here is all you have to do:

Mullein Earache Remedy

1. Put olive oil in a small jar.
2. Add my flowers to the oil. The flowers only last for one day on my stalk, so you may need to harvest flowers for several days to fill your jar.
3. Strain flowers out of oil after a few weeks.
4. Place a couple of drops of warmed oil in your ear when you have an earache.

Mullein (Verbascum thapsus)

You can tape a plant pressing on this page, draw your own plant, or make a rubbing of the plant.

Where did you find Mullein?

Second year flower stalk grows up to 7' tall. Likes full sun. Found in fields, meadows, gardens, roadside.

Elder

I am the Elder. You may have seen me growing at the edge of ponds, lakes and ditches as I love to grow where it is damp underground. In June I have groups of tiny creamy, white flowers that are in the shape of an umbrella. My leaves are long and pointy and grow opposite of one another. At the end of summer I have tasty purplish/black small berries.

My berries are good medicine! They can help prevent the flu or make an illness shorter when you do get sick from the flu. Elderberry syrup is a great way to take my medicine or you can also make a tea with my berries.

Elderberry Syrup

Ingredients:

1. 1 cup dried elderberries or two cups fresh elderberries
2. 3 cups water
3. 1 teaspoon dried cinnamon or 1 cinnamon stick
4. 1 tablespoon fresh ginger or 1 teaspoon dried ginger
5. 1 cup raw honey

Directions:

1. In a large pot, bring the elderberries, water, cinnamon, and ginger to a boil.
2. Reduce the heat, cover, and simmer until the liquid has reduced by half, about 40-45 minutes.
3. Allow the liquid to cool, and then strain
4. Press all liquid out of the berries using the back of a wooden spoon.
5. Add the raw honey and mix well. Store in a glass container in the refrigerator.

Elder (Sambucus nigra)

You can tape a plant pressing on this page, draw your own plant, or make a rubbing of the plant.

Where did you find Elder?

A shrub that grows 5'-12' and is 4'-5' wide. Likes moist soils, but will tolerate dry ground too. Full sun or part shade. Flowers in June - July Berries ripe in August - October

Glossary (New words to learn)

Plant Words:

Alternate leaves—leaves that grow alone on a stem

Berry—a small juicy fruit with the seeds inside

Buds—a small growth on a plant that grows into a leaf or flower

Bush—a woody plant that is smaller than a tree. Sometimes called a shrub as well

Forage—search for and harvest wild plants

Herb—a plant that can be used for medicine

Jagged—uneven edges on leaves

Meadow—land that is covered with wildflowers and grass

Nectar—a sweet liquid that is inside flowers, bees suck up nectar to make honey

Opposite leaves—leaves on a stem that grow across from one another

Oval—the shape of some leaves

Stem—stems grow off the main branch of the plant

Veins—transports fluid through the leaves, veins are like your blood vessels

Vine—a climbing plant

Whorled—leaves that grow in a spiral

Herb Preparation Words:

Balm—a salve made to soothe the skin

Compress—a piece of cloth soaked in an herbal infusion that is placed on skin

Glycerin—a sweet liquid made from vegetables that is used to infuse herbs into

Infusion—herbs that are soaked in a liquid

Poultice—placing plant material on the skin

Salve—an infused oil mixed with melted beeswax to thicken the oil

Strain—separate the herb material from water or oil

Syrup—an herbal infusion mixed with a sweetener like honey

Tincture—an infusion of herbs into glycerin

About the Author

Always a student of nature, Janice Marsh-Prelesnik loves to share the teachings of the nourishing and medicinal plants growing right in our backyards. Since 1981 Janice has offered the healing modalities of herbalism, home birth midwifery, massage therapy, sound healing and expressive arts/music therapy for those in hospice care. Most importantly, Janice is the mother of four grown children and is the grandmother of four amazing grand children.

What is not taught is lost in one generation.

To parents, grandparents, caregivers:

Thank you for supporting herbal education for your little one! It is my hope that this book will enhance young children's love of nature, further develop their keen observation skills, and teach basic herbal and foraging skills.

The herbs in this book are common plants that grow in the temperate regions of the world. Beginning in the springtime with Violet the book travels through the spring and late summer plants. They all be found in yards, gardens, meadows, and roadsides. Many can even be found in cities and will grow in sidewalk cracks. I have found most of these herbs in Chicago! However, due to vehicle exhaust, it is recommended that plants are NOT harvested when they grow a few feet from the road.

When foraging for medicine be sure to only take a portion of the plant growing in that area. Harvest no more than a third of the plants so that there is plenty left for regrowth.

For further herbal education for kids visit these wonderful websites:

www.learningherbs.com (specifically the Herbal Fairies educational program)
www.herbalrootszine.com (a monthly herbal education online magazine for kids)

For supplies and bulk herbs visit:

www.mountainroseherbs.com
For garden supplies and seeds:
www.richters.com
www.strictlymedicinalseeds.com

Walk gently together on the earth.

Made in the USA
Lexington, KY
28 April 2018